THE JOY OF
EASY CLASSICS

WISE PUBLICATIONS
part of The Music Sales Group

London / New York / Paris / Sydney / Copenhagen / Berlin / Hong Kong / Tokyo / Madrid

Published by
Wise Publications
14-15 Berners Street, London W1T 3LJ, UK.

Exclusive Distributors:
Music Sales Limited
Distribution Centre, Newmarket Road, Bury St. Edmunds, Suffolk IP33 3YB, UK.
Music Sales Corporation
Music Sales Corporation, 180 Madison Avenue, 24th Floor, New York NY 10016, USA.
Music Sales Pty Limited
Music Sales Pty., Units 3-4, 17 Willfox Street, Condell Park, NSW 2200, Australia.

Order No. AM1005994
ISBN: 978-1-78305-024-6
This book © Copyright 2013 Wise Publications,
a division of Music Sales Limited.

Cover illustration by Lesley Saddington.
Piano recorded by Paul Knight.
CD mixed and mastered by Jonas Persson.
Printed in the EU.

Your Guarantee of Quality
As publishers, we strive to produce every book to the highest commercial standards.
This book has been carefully designed to minimise awkward page turns and to make playing from it a real pleasure.
Particular care has been given to specifying acid-free, neutral-sized paper made from
pulps which have not been elemental chlorine bleached.
This pulp is from farmed sustainable forests and was produced with special regard for the environment.
Throughout, the printing and binding have been planned to ensure a sturdy,
attractive publication which should give years of enjoyment.
If your copy fails to meet our high standards, please inform us and we will gladly replace it.

www.musicsales.com

Air On The G String

Composed by Johann Sebastian Bach

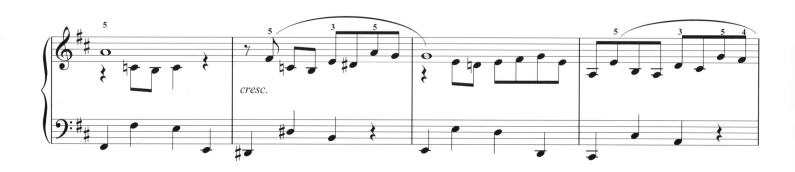

Anvil Chorus

FROM 'IL TROVATORE'

Composed by Giuseppe Verdi

2

Autumn

FROM 'THE FOUR SEASONS'

Composed by Antonio Vivaldi

3

Allegro

Ave Maria

Composed by Franz Schubert

 4 **Moderately slow**

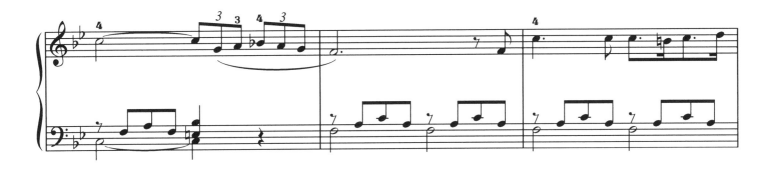

Ave Verum Corpus

Composed by Wolfgang Amadeus Mozart

5

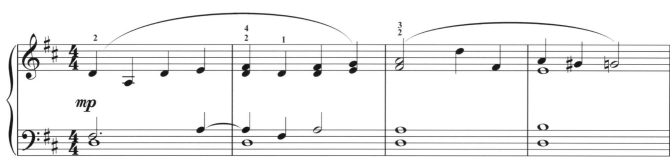

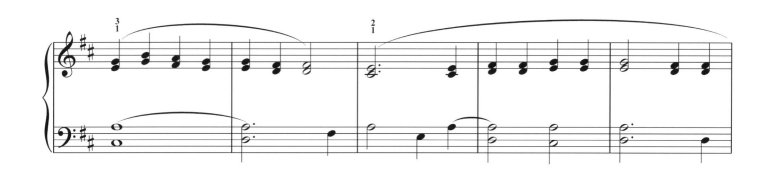

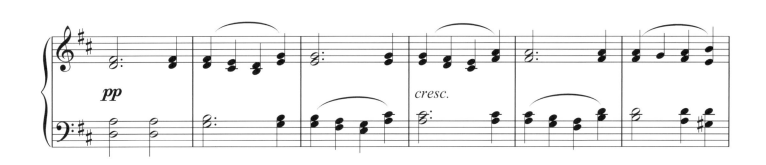

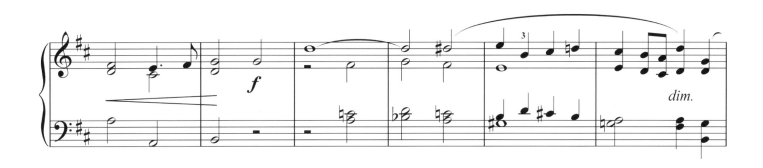

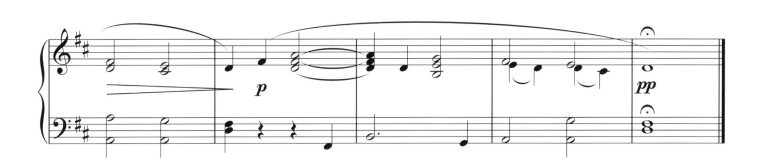

The Blue Danube

Composed by Johann Strauss Jr.

6

Fine

D.C. al fine

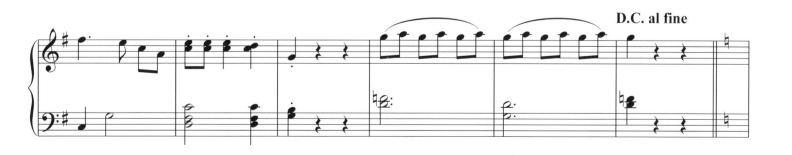

Canon in D

Composed by Johann Pachelbel

7

Moderato

Can-Can

FROM 'ORPHEUS IN THE UNDERWORLD'

Composed by Jacques Offenbach

8 **Allegro**

Cello Concerto

FIRST MOVEMENT

Composed by Edward Elgar

poco allargando

Clarinet Concerto

SECOND MOVEMENT THEME

Composed by Wolfgang Amadeus Mozart

10

Slowly

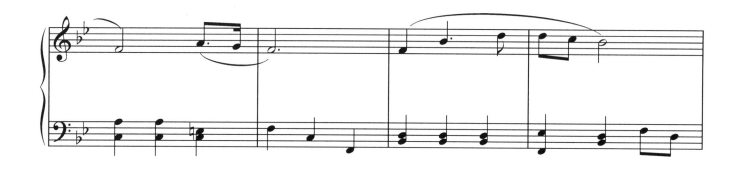

Death And The Maiden

Composed by Franz Schubert

11

La Donna è Mobile

FROM 'RIGOLETTO'

Composed by Giuseppe Verdi

12

Farandole

FROM 'L'ARLÉSIENNE'

Composed by Georges Bizet

13

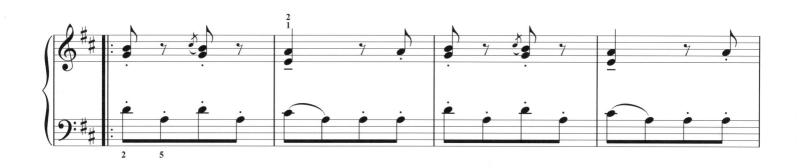

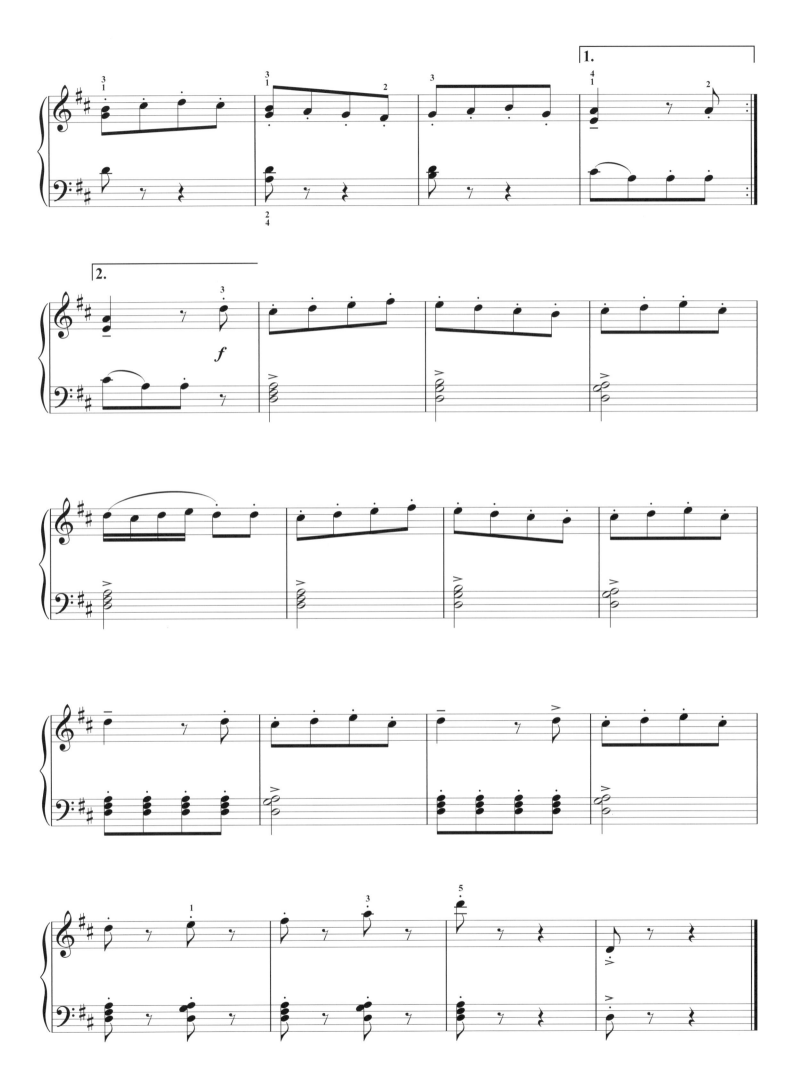

Funeral March

FROM PIANO SONATA NO.2

Composed by Frédéric Chopin

14

Flower Duet

FROM 'LAKMÉ'

Composed by Léo Delibes

15

Andantino con moto ♪ = 118

rall.

Dance Of The Sugarplum Fairy

FROM 'THE NUTCRACKER'

Composed by Peter Ilyich Tchaikovsky

 16

♩ = 108

Fingal's Cave

THEME

Composed by Felix Mendelssohn

17

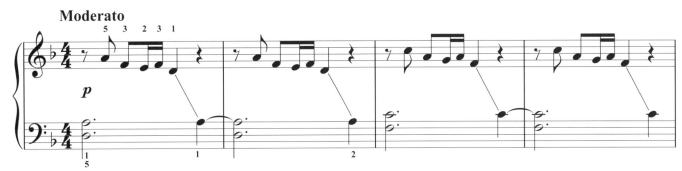

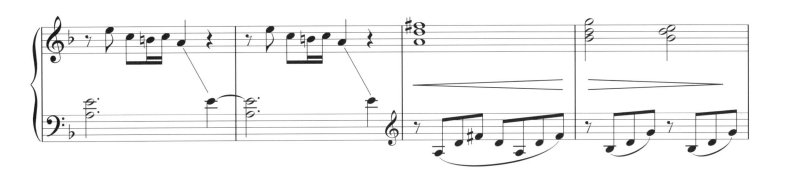

Gymnopédie No.1

Composed by Erik Satie

18

Slowly

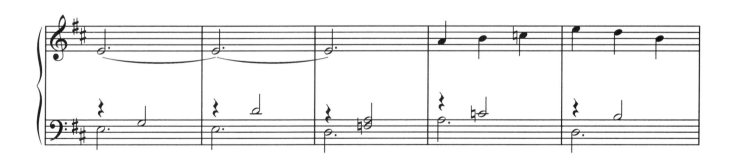

Habanera

FROM 'CARMEN'

Composed by Georges Bizet

19

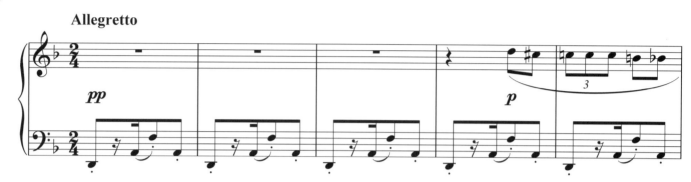

Hallelujah Chorus

FROM 'MESSIAH'

Composed by George Frideric Handel

20

Hornpipe

FROM 'WATER MUSIC'

Composed by George Frideric Handel

21

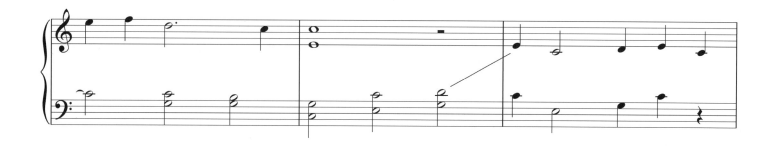

Jupiter

FROM 'THE PLANETS'

Composed by Gustav Holst

22

Moderately

Hungarian Dance No.6

Composed by Johannes Brahms

23

Minuet

Composed by Luigi Boccherini

 24

Moderato

Miserere

Composed by Gregorio Allegri

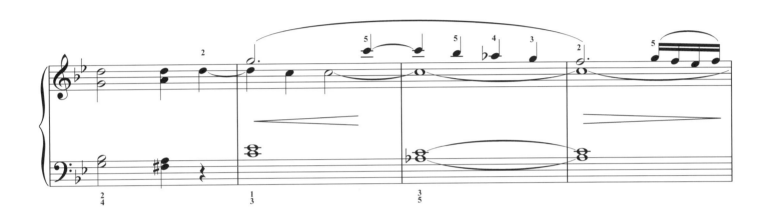

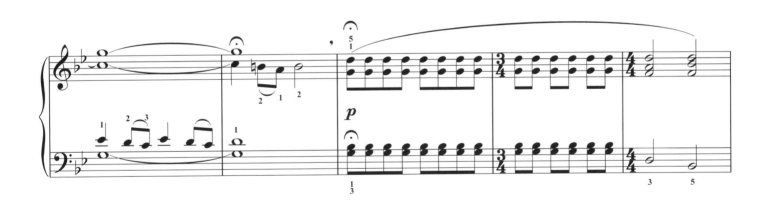

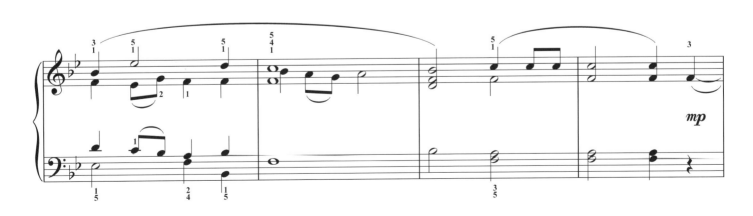

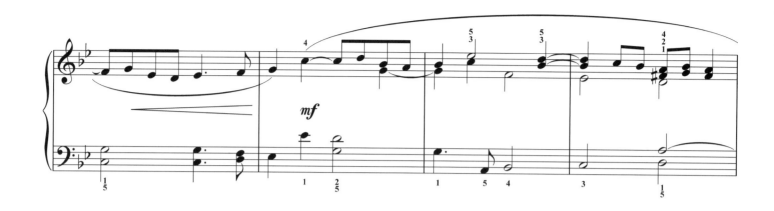

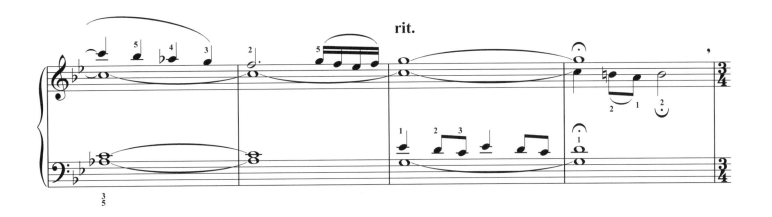

a tempo

pp *sempre*

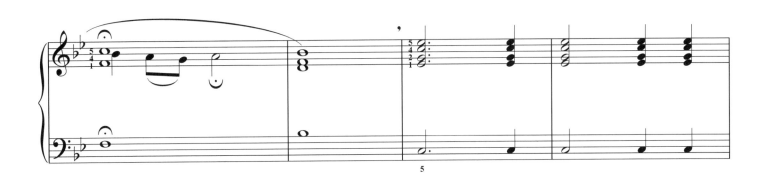

rit.

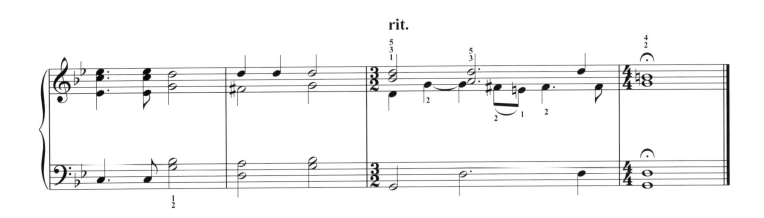

Ode To Joy

FROM SYMPHONY NO.9

Composed by Ludwig van Beethoven

26

With movement

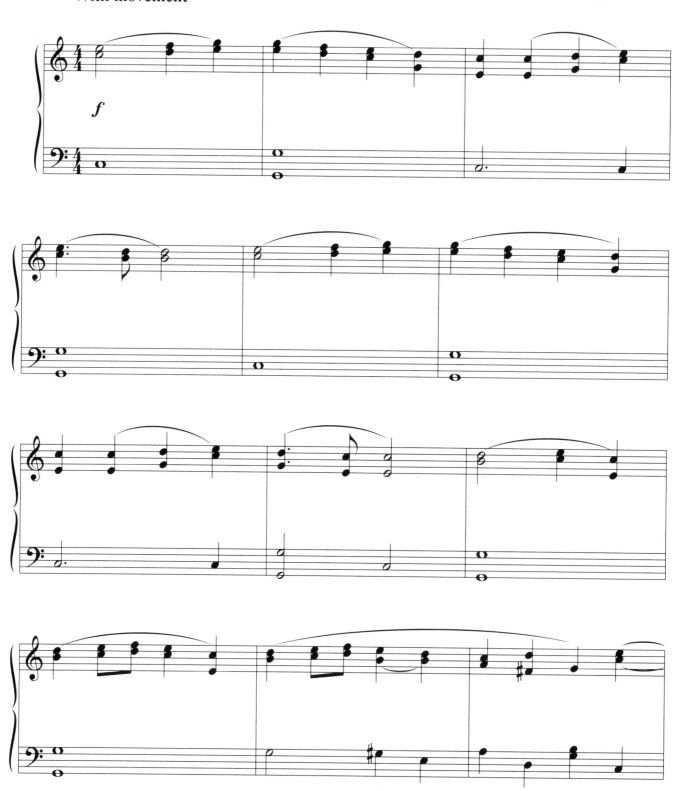

Morning

FROM 'PEER GYNT'

Composed by Edvard Grieg

27

Not too fast

Pathétique Symphony

THEME

Composed by Peter Ilyich Tchaikovsky

28

Pizzicato

FROM 'SYLVIA'

Composed by Léo Delibes

29

Polovtsian Dance No.17

FROM 'PRINCE IGOR'

Composed by Alexander Borodin

30

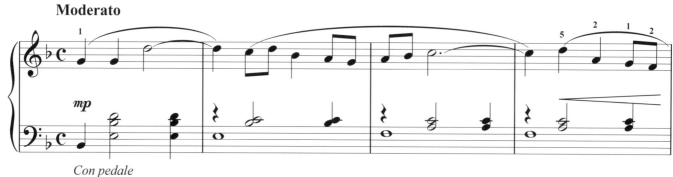

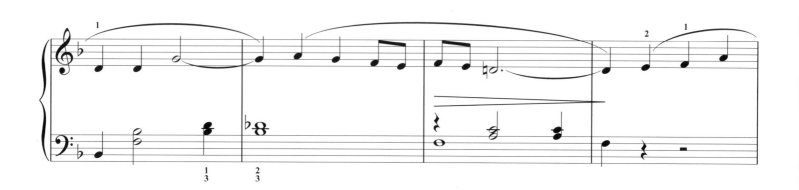

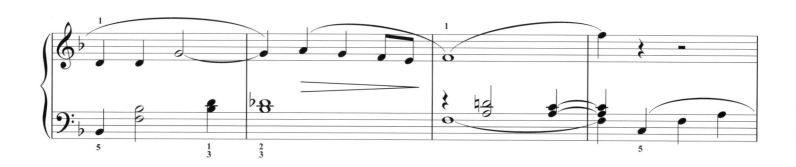

cresc. sempre

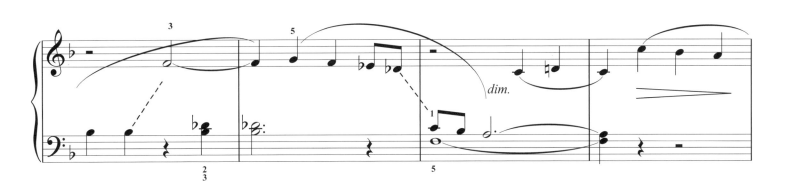

dim.

p

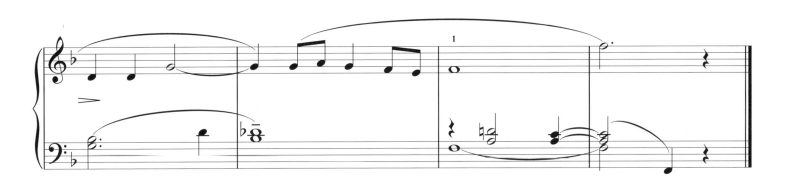

Scheherazade

'THE YOUNG PRINCE AND THE PRINCESS'

Composed by Nikolai Rimsky-Korsakov

31

'Surprise' Symphony

THEME

Composed by Franz Joseph Haydn

32

Andante

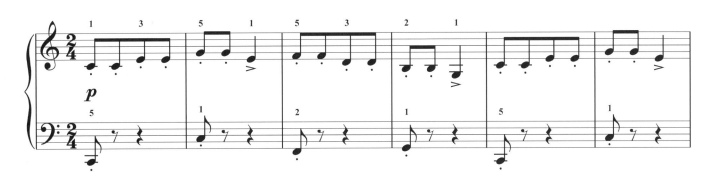

See The Conquering Hero Comes

Composed by George Frideric Handel

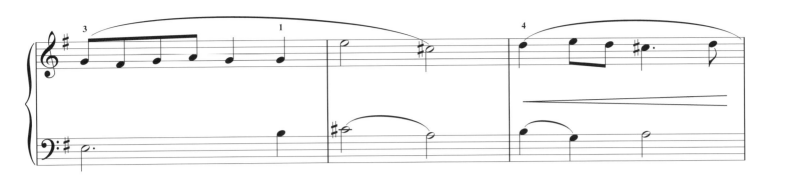

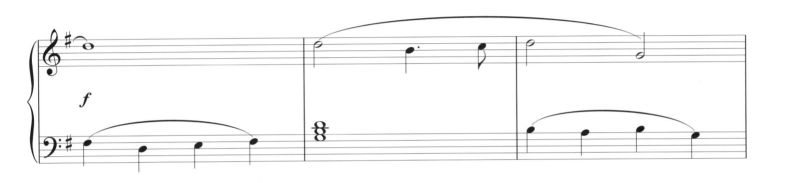

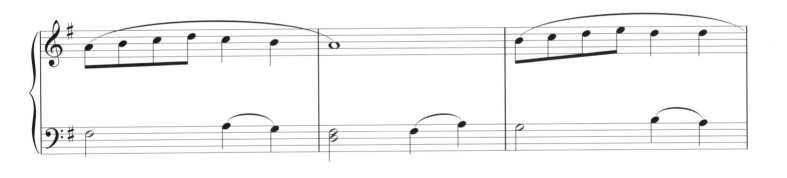

Sleepers, Awake!

Composed by Johann Sebastian Bach

34

The Swan

FROM 'CARNIVAL OF THE ANIMALS'

Composed by Camille Saint-Saëns

35

Con pedale

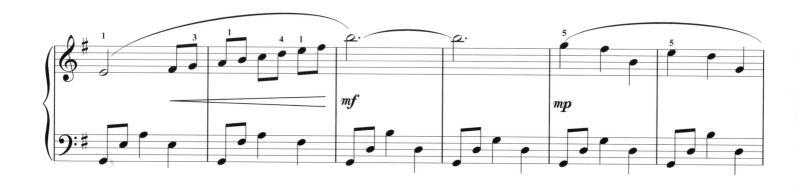

Symphony No.3

THIRD MOVEMENT THEME

Composed by Johannes Brahms

36

Poco Allegretto

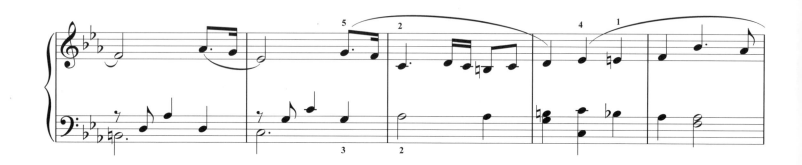

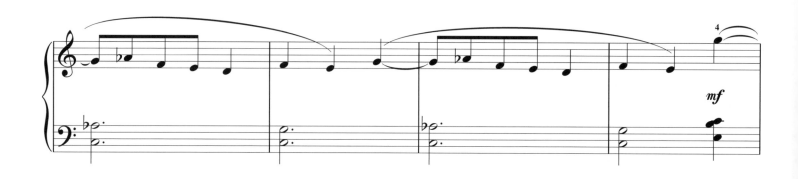

Toreador Song

FROM 'CARMEN'

Composed by Georges Bizet

37

Trumpet Tune

Composed by Henry Purcell

38

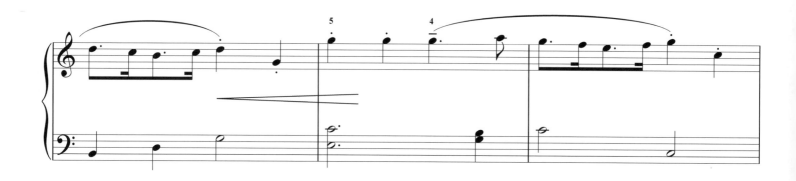

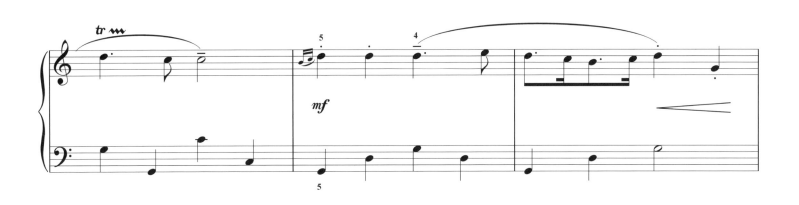

'Unfinished' Symphony

THEME

Composed by Franz Schubert

39

123456789